Order this book online at www.trafford.com
or email orders@trafford.com

Most Trafford titles are also available at major online book retailers.

© Copyright 2011 Timothy Smith Sr.

All rights reserved. No part of this publication may be reproduced, stored in a retrieval system, or transmitted, in any form or by any means, electronic, mechanical, photocopying, recording, or otherwise, without the written prior permission of the author.

Printed in the United States of America.

ISBN: 978-1-4269-7420-5

Trafford rev. 06/23/2011

Trafford PUBLISHING www.trafford.com

North America & international
toll-free: 1 888 232 4444 (USA & Canada)
phone: 250 383 6864 ♦ fax: 812 355 4082

I Am Conditioned To Go Through

By: Timothy Smith Sr.

Introduction

This is an inspirational book, to inspire, and to encourage every reader who reads this prophetic, appointed as well as anointed. It expresses everyday life experiences, and challenges that majority of us goes through in our everyday living. I have written this book for people who have low self-esteem especially those who feel like giving up. This book aims to help couples to use proper communication, and families to be encouraged not only mentally but most of all spiritually. I do realize that you can overcome, and accomplish your goal to cherish a successful life. Just remember the change starts with you.

    Finally, for the all readers of this book, I pray that this Book will comfort you in a positive way, and will give you peace of mind.

Dedication

I would like to give God the glory, who is the head of my life

my children Timothy Jr. Myra Kemari, Veronica

my sister Ebony

parents Mamie & Hayward Pastor
Bishop Eugene
Smith The Smith Family.

Dedication

In memory of my grandparent
Mamie & John Willie Smith

Ethel &William Luther Green My classmate from
medical assistance and my teacher who always encouraging
to me.

Ms.Reddin

I love you all.

Acknowledgement

I am so grateful to God in allowing me to share this book to all who will spend the time to read this amazing book. I present it to all readers who have, or may be still be experiencing some life challenges. I would like for you to take this time, and prepare yourself to see how much this book can relate to you, your family, friends, or someone that you know. This book tells you, all that I have experienced, or witnessed in my life and continue to experience as you read this anointed book of inspiration.

I would like to acknowledge some important people in my life:

First, to God, the Creator of my life.

To my parents Mamie & Hayward, thank you for all that you've done do for me.

To Ebony, my only sibling I am grateful just for who you are, don't ever change.

To my children, Timothy Jr. Myra, Kemari. and Veronica, you are my inspiration.

To my Pastor Bishop Eugene Smith who's also my uncle that I serve under as an adjutant and Seek & Find Church Family.

To My best friend Erica Burns Davis who has always been encouraging to me.

To Randolph Johnson (Poucho), thank you for your advice to stay focused.

To Aunt Gwen and Uncle Arthur Lee for all that you've done when I was out in California.

To Aunt Linda and the Gaines Family, and in Special Memory of My grandparents Mamie & John Willie Smith, Ethel & William Luther Green and to uncle Clero & Will.

Let us all be a supporter of one another because we all are important to each and everyone's life.

Chapter 1

Why am I here?

How many times have you been told that you are born in this world for a purpose? Of course you do get this remark a lot of times. But still the question remains, "What is your purpose?" and "Why are you here?" I know many of you went out of your way at one time or another to do something important or special for someone. Maybe it was a friend or even a family member. Regardless who we may have helped we are still here to serve a purpose. I believe that you will agree with me at this point. At times our life experiences make us want to stop doing when you feel like what you do is not good enough, when you are mistreated by the person or people you helped. It will make you say "Why am I here?" But the society that we live in today warrants us with so many problems that are difficult to deal with, but still we must realize that once your purpose had been identified, the next step is to refuse to be intimidated by no one in this world unless it is fearing God. Remember there is a saying that goes "You reap what you sew." Continue to keep in mind that your purpose will be accomplished regardless of what you are going through, that I am going to be steadfast unmovable and stand to accomplish my purpose for been here. Once you notice have been issue out to whatever negativities that you are facing jealousy, liar, thieves, backstabbers, to sum it all up with one word HATERS. Now that you have an idea why you are here with so many issues, let's prepare ourselves to win the war by having the right tools physically, mentally but most of all spiritually. I know that I can't change people, but I can help change my own situation. Are you ready to move on and with some more battles that you know you have a purpose? I will end this chapter with this message:

> 'Standing strong be encouraged, never give up, stay determined that I will not be defeated by the adversaries of this world, but victorious continue to become an over comer.'

Chapter 2

Finding the Peace

My own experience of trying to please others without considering my personal feelings, at times become very painful mentally as well emotionally. I learned that you can become your biggest distraction depending on the situation. I wouldn't admit how bad it hurts at first. Especially as I get older, and when I think back about my childhood and see how swiftly time have passed. I catch myself listening and helping other individuals with their problem while I ignore mine. How do you feel about those people that after you've done something and went out your way to help them and when things don't go the way she or he wants them to the bagged is brought to you the other person gets upset and will start calling names, abusing you verbally, physically or both depending on the conversation things may get heated up.

Now remember, word does hurt. It came to a point that I said to myself "never again," but still, I went against my own words and guess what? You guessed it right. I went right back to doing what I said I wouldn't do again, because I'm not at peace. Holding back that strong emotion, holding back how you really feel so that you don't explode. Because you have not let these negative thoughts leave your mind. Now you must stop, think and figure out how I find peace within myself. Yes we find different method to find peace, to sometime find out that our problem continuously repeat itself over and over again. Then something crosses your mind that you realize who all do your problem effect? Like your child or children, their school, home, someone job, or everybody period. Where is your wakeup call that made you realize to block certain things out of your life? Even though you don't forget all that has happen, there are other ways to substitute your mind for peace. As for me besides my job I go back to school taking up course in medical assistance maintain my grade with a four point zero (4.0) and stay into my studies since I already have my certification in culinary arts (professional cooking) I have other ways of thinking to keep a peace of mind and that is the future of my children hopefully that I will own a multicultural restaurant and a youth training in food service treat customers with different health illnesses. That will also allow youth to receive school credit hours. This type of mind of peace also helps me not only to think about the future of my children but also my only sibling that is young and still in school. The new mind of transition from a negative task to a positive enabled me the strength to help stay more focus to what life has to offer with the support of certain people like parents, best friends, pastor, church, teacher staff &administrators with spiritual guidance have kept me with a peace of mind. We all can have it how bad do you want it, certain things out of your life

Chapter 3

The Cost of a Dime

To you I know that a dime may seem like a small amount to pay, but it does pay off in a big way. Let me take you back to about twenty something years ago I am remember by a high school coach a of cross country running team who was practicing after school during the evening on the running track. The team were practicing for a running event that they had coming up within that same week against other teams. This team was also preparing to qualify into a conference rank for a team big national race. At this time the coach did not like what he saw in this team, so the coach told the team to stop running and form a circle were our coach had us to meet at on the track. It wants a pretty look on his face. He saw the potential that we had as a team, but saw us not trying to apply ourselves. So he asked us this question as we received our prep talk. The question was what it costs us as a team to qualify as a team. The coach replied to the team all it cost you is a **DIME**. I know you may be thinking, 'what you mean by that?' Well here it is. **D** is for dedication, you must be dedicated to the things you enjoy doing. **I** is for Interest. You must show interest into applying yourself at all times. **M** is for motivation. Stay motivated to keep your focus as a winning team and **E** is for effort, making effort to never give up until you cross the finish line. This lecture pays off big for all of us at that time to qualify for the conference, and showed us individually that a dime does have a big cost. What is it? Here it is in case you want to know again.

    Dedicated
    Interest
    Motivated
    Effort

Now are you ready to pay your dime and are you ready for your team to win the race? You apply this yourself.

Chapter 4

Wisdom of a man heart

The preparations of the heart in man and the answer from the tongue, is from the Lord. All of the ways of man are clean in his own eyes, but the Lord weighs the spirit. Commit thy works into the Lord and thy thoughts shall be established. Hand join in hand, he shall not be unpunished. By mercy and truth iniquity is purged: and by the fear of the Lord men depart from evil. When man ways please the Lord
He makes even his enemies to be at peace with him. Better is a little with righteousness than great revenues without right. A man's heart devises his way: but the Lord directs his steps. [Proverbs 16:1-9] What you can learn from this is being prepared to go through because what you're going through can causes you with blessing of overflows even when you don't see eye to eye with someone else. See when you commit yourself to the Lord. You don't have time to hate or do evil for evil. Yes we all get upset. But because God is the head of our life, the strength our joy, this why we don't has to stand in fear or worry what, going to happen to us. Who do you have trust in when you fall short? Just stay trusting in the Lord and continuing to pray for one another. If God is for us who can stand against us let nothing separate you from his love. You can be comfort. When you angry pray to him cry to him and he will be there for you. Finally say this to yourself when everyone else sees the worst in me
He [God] only sees me for who I am, He [God] doesn't judge me for what I've done, because He sees the best in me.

Chapter 5

It Was Meant Happen this Way

There is a lesson to learn for everything that we go through, it doesn't matter what it is. We often turn to making bad decision and want to blame others for our mistakes or let me say bad choices some of these bad choices that we make are being involve with alcohol a shooting dope, sex [prostitution] and much more. Now you feel like the world owes you something, because life isn't fair to you. In your mind I don't know what to do. I have too many people on my back trying to tell me how I need to live my life. But, is their something wrong for having a caring heart when they already experience more in this life than us and witness things that we haven't? When you turn on your television and you find out somebody you know were robbed and killed over five dollar, or a child, a little girl or little boy was playing in their own yard was hit in the head and killed by a stray bullet that was meant for someone else. Now someone is trying to help you, but oh know you are ready to start using profanity fight yell and scream still what have you solve. Have you tried to stop to examine your own life on how you are living your life and if so, have you asked yourself am I really satisfied with my lifestyle? If not what areas in my life do I need to improve on or to better at, before you start criticizing somebody else wrong doings? Knowing that you are only hurting yourself. You must get set into your mind that I am tired of being tired in other words; I don't want to live the way that I am living any more. No therapy, medication, church, or any other spiritual guidance will be able to help you until you are ready to help yourself. First you stop being in denial admit that you have a problem now if you're getting this message say to yourself I am ready for my change. Okay let's begin to remember I stated earlier your problem will still exist until you are ready to make the transition in other words change in you. Next is to find the resources where you can go and get help with. Now it's time for the research to begin. How do you know when the change is in you? This is how. When your determination becomes your denominator to dominate any situation that you face with, having spiritual resource is the best resource. It energizes me prepare for my obstacles that I sometimes has to face. The mastering change in you happen when you know that your past is always going to be thrown up in your face, but when it no longer affects you to react negatively with your old habits, then you know that you are progressing and part of your goal is

achieved.
    It will now allow you to witness to help others who is now going through what you has overcome to help the next individual, and take a look back to understand why your situation is meant to happen this way.

Chapter 6

You are welcome in this place

Hello everyone welcome to a place where you don't has to be a stranger there's help all over this place. There's no right or wrong answer just don't be stupid to the question you hold back that can be answered .And to let you know mother is here in the building to make sure no one don't get out of line. Does everyone have their working tools there's no excuses we don't accept them in this department. Now everyone take out your working material because the boss is ready to give instruction are you ready. In this place you can express your needs, concern and personal matter it is safe because the boss' love this the best because the job is ensure of getting done the boss don't have to look over her back. Why? Yes you said because mother keeps everyone in order she is well respected. When it's time for reports, our shift looks for nothing but an excellent report again because of mother. Now it's time to go on break, going for lunch. Mother makes sure everyone is okay later there seem to be a dispute, guess who stepped in? Somebody says mother, well you're right. Because another employ don't like some of our crew mother lets everyone that they has job to do and refuse to allow her crew get fire over something petty. Everything calm down and everyone is back to work mother lecture her crew once our shift has ended for today we all break down our machine and prepare for another day everyone is at peace because mother know about how to keep everything in order with no confusing at the end of the day everyone is happy. Now do you see while you are welcome in this place because we all have six month before retirement.

It's time to start our shift. Everyone has taken their materials that is needed the boss has

Mrs. Gilda MOTHER OF OUR CLASS

My Medical Assistance Instructor Ms. M. Reddin

Chapter 7

Healthy Communication for a Healthy Relationship

We all use communication in many ways, so let's get ready for a very exciting lesson that we all can learn to better ourselves. First communication start with you the first technique that I would like to start with is finding the right time to talk: Since communication start with you first finding the right time regardless if it dealing with you ,a mate or family choosing the right time to talk is very important So that everyone who is involve is calm, stress free, and not distracted. This is the first way of resolving issues through communication, or a healthy relationship. Now let's take a look at the second techniques.

Try to put yourself in the other person place. It is very easy to blame each other when you want to get your point across. Again remember the first part of communication. By putting yourself in the other person place allow both individual to try and understand each other issues without one trying to prove the other person wrong. This technique is for you to be a solution to the problem instead of adding to the problem. Now let's take a look at the third technique. Help each other stay motivated. Hopefully so far I hope that you are learning to become a better communicator. This third technique of communication is something that affects you in a positive way and helps keep you going. You with goals set for yourself, mate, or family by both coming to an agreement that will help you accomplish your goal or goals. The next four techniques will be discussed in the next chapter.

Chapter 8

Healthy Communication for a Healthy Relationship (Continuation)

Hopefully these techniques on healthy communication for healthy relationship are being helpful for you as you take a look at some of your own issues today. I am sure by you applying yourself to use these techniques will help make a difference for your situation.

Now let's take a look at technique number four, Staying reminded of yourself.

Staying reminded of yourself: Remember never to hold anything that you are feeling it's very important to lay everything out on the table to express what is on your mind to whomever the issues of the matter to whom it contains to. Be expressive, or put spoken without causing a conflict but be honest to yourself. This is the most important person that matter out of the whole equation.

Now it's time for technique number five let's see what it is.

Active Listener: This next technique is a main problem that majority of us have, what do you think it is? Still thinking, well let's just let it be known. Our main problem is we just need to shut up. Say it with me, Shut up! Majority of the time we are so interesting in just trying to get our point across by just trying to prove how the other person was wrong instead of trying to understand that's not always the case sometimes to be an active listener never interrupt, give advice, or try to make the other person look or feel bad. The individual that is doing the speaking or being spoke to let them have the spotlight by just not saying nothing. What does that mean again? Just Shut Up! It doesn't mean that you always done something wrong sometime a person just want you to listen, or the other way around. It's another way of saying just want to be heard. This is the importance of being active listener. I believe that majority of us can agree.

The next technique is number six It's Mutual.

It's Mutual: This technique is really plain and simple to just be yourself that really go back to technique number four. There is no need to try to impress other out of stupidity to try to let someone's attention you don't has to try to prove yourself to people just stay open minded and be yourself and to take it one day at time.

    Now the last technique is rewarding yourself.
    Rewarding Yourself; As we all have learn it does take time working on communication in order to have a healthy relationship, remember there is no perfect relationship, and there never will be, but going through these six techniques at the end there is another wrong with rewarding yourself by acknowledging all of your obstacle that you has overcome. I am encouraging you to stay positive and know you can make a difference.

Chapter 9

Journey On

Here I am in a place knowing not what tomorrow may bring, I am flying out on this journey where will I land at, is the big question that still remain with me. I already am told that this journey was not going to be easy. But I have decided to journey on to see what the end going to be. Now, I must say there has being plenty of turbulence, while traveling on this journey, but I still journey on. I have landed in a strange place of the unknown this place is wild, life threatening, still not knowing what tomorrow is going to bring. I am out here at times feeling that I'm all alone, still I journey on. I came across all types of people to just name a few liars, thieves, hopeless, backsliders, but still I journey on. I will admit I have also come across some good people as well there were encouraging, grace, and mercy, also great was with Thou faithfulness, while morning shine so bright. Still I journey on. I will let you know as I continue travel on this journey I being lied on, talk about, criticizes of things that I did not do, But yes still I journey on. I am out here still on this journey there was some amazing things that has still continue to happen to me it had me running for my life. There are so many things going through my mind, I remain not knowing what tomorrow will bring but still journey on. I'm a lot further out on this journey then what is expected, Oh yes still with a long way to go, how long I don't know.in case you still wonder where am I at this point, still I journey on. I'm must continue to still run on to see what the ends going to be. Out here I come to realizes that it is all about surviving that I was glad to run back into faith family hope, be encourage, fear not, trusting in the Lord finally got me to the end of my journey when I saw the rainbow

    I thought about the flood of Noah and the Ark, but instead it was my destination. And heard a voice that stated to me well done my servant. You has taken this journey very wise all the way to the end, through my obedience I welcome you with open arms your journey has being accomplish. You has journey on into paradise where you will spent eternity. Now journey on.

Chapter 10

Because Of Who You Are

I am so, grateful because of who you are, bright, intelligent regardless of how things may seems to be, you never let the relationship change between you, or me. You still remain to be just who you are. I always love you for being their in a time of needs That ear to listen, eyes to observe, without judgment, but most of all understanding of godly wisdom whenever I'm going through you told me just put God first in all things I do. I know if he did it for me he will do the same for you.

So continue on this day don't change, because my God will guide you the right way, and never ever lead you astray. He knows the pain of your suffering scars, but most of all about the type person you serve to be, just because of who you are.

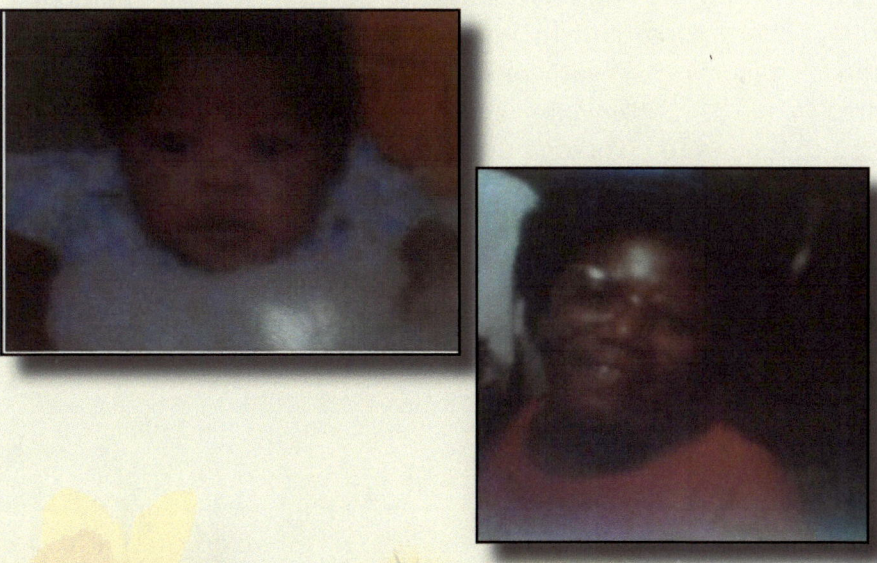

Chapter 11

I Fell Down but I Got Up

We all get into many situation where we fell, some of us get up, other stay down. Yes a fall can hurt depending on hard that you fall it can make you bleed and live a scar for life. This the way our life is for some of us we have falling into some bad situation that we are trying to get up from. Doesn't allow yourself to go paralyzes, in other words helpless to the point that we are not able to function. There is too many of us that just use our past for an excused that we allow ourselves not to move forward. I say to you again don't let your life become paralyzes. There comes a times when you just need to grow up I know that this may seem harsh but think about how many opportunities you has giving up on what you could be doing. But yet complaining about why you were unable to do something that you never tried. How many of you have degrees but yet still complain about why you can't get a job because it doesn't pay you enough, and have or some mouth that you need to feed. Stop using too many excuses. Get up off the floor, Go freshing up get out the door and go take care of your business. Think about every person life including that you have an effect on including you. This is the first person that it starts with. Whatever area that you have fallen at remember that you can get up. There is area in our life were we have left trash that we need to sweep up and throw into the trash, also trash that need to be taken out that is already fill up and ready for the dumpster. In other words some of us have too much drama like baby mommy, issued It's time or let me say it's being time to stop being ride on like a donkey. Think about everyone who depends on you and ask yourself this I fell down, will I stay down for all of those who I am responsible for keep or using my pass for an excuse or get up and tell all those love ones my life is in your hands. Get up!

Chapter 12

Just Do The Right Thing!

Many of us make choices in life that we often regret to find yourself saying if I only would had listened. But it's ok it's not the end of the world, only if we don't try to learn from our own mistake I know that I am about to step on some toes, if I do don't get mad just say ouch!!! People allow too much from their past stand in the way of their future, now you know that is not right, so you let someone else take your joy. When you do the right thing plenty of things happen allow me to mention a few. people will criticize you when because there's greatness inside of you, you don't you know this type of jealous from the enemy bring on an attack against you even though you haven't done anything to anyone the question that I ask do you really has to do anything to anyone for them to attack? I think not, Because of jealousy again this what happens. The enemy will try to press you down knowing that you already heard of the saying that misery love company, So at this point you don't has to fall into the trap of the wicked but caution go knowing with your spiritual faith in God the enemy cannot defeat you because you are a conquer. Once that have being establish how you are living you can weigh what you need to be corrected in your life. Lots of times we are too quick to here and slow to speak just wait by faith, and be a good example setter. We already know that there are consequences to pay for when you do the wrong thing. So you can imagine what happen just to the right things. No one should be able to intimidate
you if you are strong mighty now don' get it twisted I did say if you are strong minded to where you is not intimidated then it is not difficult for you to do the right thing I do know that you will be challenge, but where is your faith to hold on, be staying encourage and just do the right thing.

Chapter 13

A True Believer

A true believer never doubts

Accepts all challenges in life without a fight

Because spiritually this battle that you are in is not yours

But it is the Lord, According to the master plan

That all favors are in your hand

Now that you know that you will never ever has to fail

Because when you are a child of God,

All of his children always prevail.

That's only because of the type of person that I am

And just in case you ask who am I this will be my reply

A true believer that's who I am! Again ask me who am I,

A TRUE BELIEVER THAT'S WHO I AM, A TRUE BELIEVER THAT'S WHO I AM!!!

Chapter 14

To Whom It May Concern

Listen help to this messages it may contain some very important information that may be able to you through your circumstances if don't apply to you, then don throw it away give it to someone that you know that can benefit from it. Today we have given up opportunities in our life because we don't apply ourselves. Just waiting for things to be handed to us. I don't mean to be cruel, so just allow me to keep everything real. Lots us don't achieve our opportunity because of one word lazy. We depend on a system as a escape. And uses excuses to why we cant do something we never tried, complaining the job don't pay enough that is willing to hire you with o qualification. I haven't forgotten about you qualified candidate that's complaining about your education or degrees that is hanging around some where getting dusty because things don't operate around your schedule so what, Some of us sat around too long giving off of our child or children money, Then uses God understand my situation. He been understood your problem when it first started that still exist in lots of us today. We sit back on the things that we should be doing. And do other things that we already now not to do. So who fault is it because you cant have your way all the times. People remember you cant make for the time that's already gone. But yes you can for the one you're in now that will pass over into another day of opportunity for you to become a achiever for all that's precious to share, or sit back in your do nothing lazy boy chair. Let all strive to do better. If this message in this letter was for you, or again To Whom It May Concern.

Chapter 15

Encourage Yourself

Whatever is true,

Whatever is noble,

Whatever is right,

Whatever is pure

Whatever is lovely,

Whatever is admirable

if anything is excellent or praise worthy think about such things(philippians4:8)
Knowing who you are, not letting anything tears you apart
Show your confident in having faith, and trusting
what you believe in does for you, and how it
can bring you close together like family.
So yes encourage yourself I do

Chapter 16

Going To The Other Side

Sitting back relaxing on the couch planning out what will I do today? what will the weather be like. I just don't know. While I'm here figure out your full schedule of a daily assignment, It might be to take a trip out of town whatever you decides to do make it worthwhile, For we spend so much time working and paying bills that most of us rarely get the opportunity to explore new activities in this world we should be able every once in a while to travel to another side of life, a week cruise to a Island of your choice, spa, or some type of relaxation, resort, just treating yourself to something good. Experiencing different styles of living is an excellent experiment, to travel places that you never being before .Keep a journal, and share it with your child, children, grandchildren, grandparent, and etc. We only live once on this earth some times we need to make it be about us, only in a positive way. There are time you just need the break it releases stress or thing that has being heavy your mind. Spending that time wisely can mean al to just try to make a schedule that you can have a retreat get away for your self at least three time out the year or more remember here on earth we only live once. Explore by going to the other side of the world that you never travel to before and treat yourself.

Chapter 17

Trouble Doesn't Last Always

I am reminded of a song that says I'm so glad that trouble doesn't last always. Now we all have fallen into some type of trouble, one way of another and if you haven't keep on living. Now living in these time and days it's not all good, but it's not all bad. Be thankful either way because your enemy can help your trouble days become your break through .I am convinced that you are spiritual protected from the enemy. The enemy is warned about trying to attack you. Just read these words of your protection. The Lord is my light and my salvation who shall I fear? The Lord is the strength of my life whom shall I be afraid? When the wicked .even mine enemies and my foes, came upon me to eat up my flesh, They stumble and fell, Though a host shall encamp against me, my heart shall not fear though war should rise up against me, in this will I be confident. That one thing that may have I desired of the Lord, that I will seek after; that I may dwell in the house of the Lord all the days of my life, to behold the beauty of the Lord, and to enquire in his temple. For in the time of trouble he shall hide me in his pavilion in the secret of his tabernacle shall he

 I will sing, yea, I will sing unto the Lord. Hear Oh Lord When I cry with my voice have mercy also upon me and answer me when thou seek thou face. Thy face I will seek Hide not thy face far from me put not thy servant away in anger thou has been my help; leave me not; neither forsake me; Oh God of my salvation. When my mother and father forsake me, then the lord will take me up. Teach me thy way Oh Lord will take me up teach me thy way oh Lord and lead me in the plain path, because of mine enemies. Deliver me not over to the will of my enemies. For false witnesses are risen up against me. Such as breathe out cruelty. I have fainted, unless I had believed to see the goodness of the Lord.in the land of the living. Wait on the Lord; be of good courage and he shall strengthen thine heart. Wait I say on the Lord. This protection guarantees your victory.

Chapter 18

You Can't Stop Me

This is a mission to that foundation that's ready to go way out and beyond, the takeoff is about to begin are you ready for the count down 10,9,8,7,6,5,4,3,2,1,0. Takeoff no turning back until mission is accomplished. You are held accountable for your ammunition, every individual will have their own battle, so be prepared, your battle can come at any time, I am ready for this. Well mine has just begun, misery, and company. They are lover in case you didn't know, their job is to make your life a living hell, whatever it takes if dealing with your finance, family, job, and etc., lots of time the fire get hatred up that other things get involve like the police, ambulance, courts, I ask myself why me, I don't deserve this, falsely accuse, persecuted, What's next now, You were warn about this mission, are you ready to give up. I don't think so there is so many things that have giving me a advantage on how to complete this mission first you has to have a refuse to give up attitude, in other words You Can't Stop Me! Bring on, I have a foundation that will not be destroyed. So your foolishness will be ignored, because this intermission that is inside of me has me protected, with prayer. It gives me strength day by day that never ever loses its power. It is discipline with determination and motivation just come too far to turn around, it can take punches, because it knows that you shall reap what you sew and what you do to me is already done back to you, so now the mission is a battle you have the ammunition that is for you since every one of us has a different mission. If we don't have the same ammunition at least we should find something in common, to complete our mission. That I see I can continue on now. To do what need to be done,

I just received the call by using my ammunition I came out on top. You can to. Find your You Can't Stop Me

ammunition.

Chapter 19

Touch Up

Touch up in the area of your room that's needed touching up it may be a area where you may need to leaves some friends alone just come out of your comfort zone to allow yourself to go that you have never gone before. Touching up can give you a better look on your appearance on how to make better decision on past mistake, not to say that more want be made but you can avoid from making the same repeat. Shine with a new look that gives you extra lasing confident comfortable soul that's a cleanser treatment to fix up the damages with full coverage

Touch up to stand up to the heat and humidity of this evilness that's in this world. Always feeling fresh and flexible. Ok it depends on your mood, your touch may change with the season, constantly changing all year round to match your touch; so get your best result. With a touch up through the rough area of your livestock up where ever is needed. The touch is in you don't let it go no not perfect just strive for that inspiration of wisdom to carry on. One extraordinary touch is recognized about what has taken place, and that is another chance for me to start all over again not focus on what part of the area of my life that has being damage but the area that can get repaired. That's the touch up.

Chapter 20

Get Over It

Get over it it's over now there no need for anybody finger pointing just accept that fact that it just over. I say this today to all of you know what to expect, Get over it, Yes I said get over it because tomorrow will bring a better you a better me. Dwelling back past cost nothing but more conflict toward the situation unless you are thinking about reconciliation, Get over it. Everyone get hurt in some type of way the healing process start, when you learn that, you start with thinking positive things that need to take place with you to Get over your issues as well as the other individual. Don't be distracted from someone else stupidity effect your success for living, You can get over it By not participating in the conversation, just stay away from having contact or discussion to anyone again to avoid conflict. So that everyone can now move forward.

Chapter 21

What Time Is It?

Those of you that are a football should be familiar with this quote "what time is it?" What time is it?" "What time is it?" There is plenty to discuss about the importance of time.

It's time to be aware of family time, It's time for everyone to take their responsibility, and accept their own actions, spiritual get a connection to their community and support healthy choices with their behavior. Using your unique ability to contribute to the positive well being environment says a lot about you. To take the time showing interest helping to make a difference.

Being open for change allow the communication time for all these thing below, take a look
Time to express your concern of what's on your mind.
Time to care and give freely,
Time to respect, and show respect toward one another.
Time to be affectionate
Time to spend that quality time that needed for the family, most of all for yourself
Time can be established in so many go ways when we use time wisely. I am reminded that you can't make up for the time that's gone only the time that is now. So time does end at some giving point. Right now it's your time, my time, mourning time to take back what you have allow to get away, take the time to get back the life of the dream that can still be achieved before that time end.

Chapter 22

Keep Holding On

Sitting back thinking on what to do after all that I am going through not forgotten, the struggle the pain the misery that I feel inside, Why me? I ask myself overhand over again, The cruelty of some people that you go out your way for now this the type of thank you that I get from you. Where do I go from here I ask myself. The is clear keep holding on because the trouble don't last always don't you know that it was a set up for to go through, and here it is you is wondering why b because of your season being harvest to multiply your blessing of break through that you though were counted out. Never gave up always willing to go the extra miles through the affliction. But you keep holding on why because something inside of me telling me to go ahead whatever I will just continue to keep my peace, in the midst of this storm I being told to hold on to God unchanging hand, live by his command, cause everything is going to be all right. Keep holding on my brother; Keep holding on my sister, why again because you is being process for your season is near, keep holding on and don't you never give up.

Chpater 23

Victory Is Mine

Fighting for what you believe in, refusing to give up, can be a victory depending on what ground. It let others know that you can't be push around. Having a set mine that is stable to protect what's yours, because I am somebody, who will be respected, not neglected.

I am determine, to whole my own, I want be treated any type of way. I will let you know when the line is cross the wrong way. I am a man, not only by age, a Father not only by a title. I'm not your boy, and refuse to allow you to call me onetime not impress by the crowd that you entertain for cheers and a laugh, Your childish ways is already defeated, this victory is mine because the evilness of your ways is known and monitor none is worry but is caution in case you decide to push the wrong button, you will be destroy. Focus on getting alone instead of criticism toward one another we all in the same boat together where I can help you, and you can help me, This don't has to be a war. The foolishness can end at any time, whatever you decide, just still, remember victory is mine.

Chapter 24

What's The Word?

There word is identified in many expects, some are recognizes as something being said, as a sound another states a series of speech, sounds that communicates, a meaning. a graphic of representation, a order command, person of the Trinity, gospel news, the verb acknowledge that it is express in words as you can see t he word is vision on these level physically, emotionally, mentally, and spiritually, here the term of the word expresses its different styles of communication. I want you to see it this way, inspirational

First I believe we can accept the word as Wisdom,

Wisdom: being wise, learning knowledge, good sense, insight, judgment wise with action, next word, Observance worthy, capable of being watchful, mindful, gather proper information next word, Revealing always noticeable, in site, never hiding from the last word,

Delighted highly please, gratified, and pleasurably satisfied in its work.

from the spiritual view the word is a creator, that created things also spoke words into existence, and remain life living, that once dwell in a human body as you can see the word is powerful, real, and still exist. Hopefully by now you has received and accepted this word.

Chapter 25

One Day at A Time

Listening to your parent telling how they grew up from their past, is very interesting, especially when we take a look at today society, new technology, that have taken place over this world has cost many of us jobs, homes, now is affecting our child, or children education. No I won't go into talking politics even though its a struggle. My mother and her sibling with little education, but they knew how to survive, with having a big family no one was never in need, because people back then believe I helping out each other, there were more family value, respect.

People got along better with another not saying that they didn't have problem

I was also reminded what happen when your parent was not around, If you did something wrong around another adult who knew your parent, they were to discipline you, they would let your parent know, and you got discipline by your parent and it wont child abuse, just a way of showing tough love. Now today the appreciation of our parent should be respected from their past experience growing up through hard time help me with spiritual motivation of my own personal problem. If you were to ask them how did they get through their hard time I believe that they will go back to their spiritual value and say I took one day at a time. I know you heard of that saying and that song I have aunt name Linda that bring tears to my eyes when I heard her sang that song. That helps me to make it day by day when

say Lord give me the strength to do everything that I has to do, yesterday gone sweet Jesus and tomorrow may never be mines, but Lord for my sake help me to take one day at a time and that's a message good enough for me to live by everyday.

MY UNCLE AND AUNT LINDA WHO IS AN
EXCELLENT SINGER BESIDE MAKING EVERYONE
FAVORTIE DESERT